Big Tan Van

Written by Sharon Wohl
Illustrated by Lisa Bradley

A Better Way of Learning
Creator of The Phonics Game™

Printed in the U.S.A.

A Better Way of Learning • *www.phonicsgame.com*

Big tan van.
Bob gets in.

Pam, Ben, Tim, Dot
and Bud get in.

Pets get in.

Jan, Wes, Sis,
Tom, Russ,
Pat, Bev, Kim,
Don and
Gus get in.

Bob tells Kit,
"Stop!"

but Kit gets in.

Flats!

Pets get off.
Kids get off.

Big, tan, sad van.